Can I Retire?

Your Personal Guide To Retirement

By Ken Mahoney

First edition.

ISBN-13: 978-0-9828887-0-4

This publication contains the opinions and ideas of the author. It is sold with the understanding that neither the author nor publisher is engaged in rendering legal, tax, investment, insurance, financial, accounting, or other professional advice or services. If a reader requires such advice or services, a competent professional should be consulted. References to organizations have been given for the purpose of information and do not constitute a recommendation. Any perceived slights of specific people or organizations are unintentional.

No warranty is made with respect to the accuracy or completeness of the information contained herein, and both the author and publisher specifically disclaim any responsibility for any liability, loss or risk, personal or otherwise, which is incurred as a consequence, directly or indirectly, of the use of any of the contents of this book. While the information and advice in this book are believed to be accurate and true at the time of publication, neither the author, publisher or distributor can guarantee results nor accept any responsibility or liability for any damage or losses of any kind resulting from any advice included in this guide, be it from the author, any person or persons mentioned in this book, or any product, listing or mention, whether directly or indirectly.

TABLE OF CONTENTS

ABOUT THE AUTHOR—KEN MAHONEY

With over 22 years of professional experience, Ken Mahoney, owner of Mahoney Asset Management, is an accomplished financial advisor, author, and speaker.

Ken sat on the Advisory Board of the House of Representatives Banking and Finance Committee, has taught finance at Dominican College, and won the 2001's annual "Stock Picking" contest held by Gannett Newspapers. He is a frequent guest speaker at various business associations, corporations, senior groups, and other organizations throughout the region.

His expertise has not gone unnoticed by the periodicals either, as his opinions on the world of finance have been published nationally. Ken's market comments and perspectives are published in the Hudson Valley Business Weekly and his financial opinions have been published by USA Today, as well as by various local publications. He is a familiar quoted figure in the business pages of The Journal News and was a respected member of the newspaper's Business Leaders Roundtable.

Ken Mahoney is the creator of the Westchester Stock Index and the Rockland Stock Index, both of which have appeared in a number of newspapers.

Ken hosted WRKL Radio's Smart Investor show from 1992 to 1998, and co-hosted Financial Mobility on WRKL and TKR. He also hosted "Invest in You Community" in the early 1990s. Since 1992, Ken has published the financial newsletter, "The Smart Investor".

He has earned distinguished service awards from the NY State Legislation, County of Rockland, and NY State Assembly for his work with charities. As a respected leader in the community, Ken has chaired United Way special events and is currently the Co-Chair of the Business Council of the Make-a-Wish Foundation of Hudson Valley, a foundation that helps raise funds to support the mission of granting wishes to children. His efforts as co-chairperson of the foundation's gala events helped raise substantial funds to further the organization's goals and he and his wife have been honored at past Galas.

Ken also served for seven years as a member of the Board of Directors for Meals on Wheels and has been involved in the agency's golf and tennis challenge. Meals on Wheels honored Ken as "Rockland's Community Leader of the Year" in 2002. He is now on the Board of Richmond Community Services, which aims to provide support to people and their families with developmental disabilities.

Ken is co-publisher and writer of The Rockland Business Digest in the spring of 2006. Every issue is sent to 11,000 businesses and has over 70,000 monthly website hits.

Ken is also the author of "Investing From Within: A Story of Understanding", which offers investment advice to various personality types; a series entitled "The Zoo Exchange: Teaching Our Kids About Money", which teaches children about finance principles; and "Now What? A Guide To Retirement During Volatile Times", a book that focuses on protecting your capital, making tax efficient distributions, and transferring your wealth in the most economical way.

You can catch Ken giving a market report every morning on WRCR 1300am at 9:15am (www.wrcr.com and www.WTBQ.com).

Ken has been married for 17 years to his wife, Trish, and has two sons, Brendon and Connor, for whom he coaches baseball and soccer.

THIS PAGE HAS BEEN INTENTIONALLY LEFT BLANK

THIS PAGE HAS BEEN INTENTIONALLY LEFT BLANK

DEDICATION

This book is dedicated to all my clients who have entrusted Mahoney Asset Management to help them plan for their futures. I also appreciate the friendships I have made with each and everyone one of them.

To the future...

The mission of Mahoney Asset Management
Know our clients well
Anticipate their need
Exceed their expectations!!

THIS PAGE HAS BEEN INTENTIONALLY LEFT BLANK

PREFACE

When thinking about retirement a lot of people think about the value of their brokerage accounts, retirement accounts, annuities, life insurance and what they expect to receive from social security. But they tend not to think as much about how much income they will need in retirement and how much income their savings will generate.

After compiling the balances from your investments you may feel quite comfortable with the final figure but have you also included any debt, perhaps a mortgage payment and/or a college loan? And have you considered how much your expenses will be?

While many books discuss retirement in terms of accumulating wealth, it is equally important to consider how you see yourself in retirement – where you would like to live, what activities you would like to pursue and the associated costs. Once you understand what you want in terms of lifestyle, I think you'll start looking forward to answering the question, "Can I retire?"

Can I retire? Most people today make that decision predicated on their financial situation. But there are other components of retirement I would like you to consider. Most importantly, I would like you to consider having purpose in your life during retirement.

The transition of going from working to retirement or from structured to non-structured can be difficult. So it's important to "transfer" the structure of the "work world" to your own new structure of retirement.

I am always amazed by the number of people who have told me how they looked forward to retirement – no more commuting, no more early/late meetings, no more deadlines – only to realize, once retired, they really did enjoy working. So while you contemplate your retirement and whether or not can you retire financially, you should really start laying out some goals and objectives for yourself during your retirement. I suggest sitting down with pen and paper and identifying some of the things you would like to in retirement including what is necessary to actually do them.

Many people find it difficult to make the transition from pre-retirement to retirement. They are used to getting up at 7:00 a.m. destined for the office by 9:00 a.m. with a full schedule of meetings, projects and to-dos but when that alarm clock doesn't go off they find themselves somewhat at a loss of what to do next.

I hope, by now, you realize this book is not just about financing your retirement or meeting with your accountant or your investment advisor. Thinking about and planning for your retirement should not just be about the numbers. Thinking about and planning for your retirement should also be thoughtful and mindful of where and how you see yourself and your future.

Most people claim "Of course I want to retire, I can't wait to retire". But you really need to think about all that it encompasses – from the basic necessities like shelter, food and clothing to the more elaborate like travel, hobbies and gifting.

Many people, well into their 80's and 90's, continue to work because they enjoy what they do. I know an attorney who is now 82 years old and just enjoys work and helping others. He doesn't work 12 hour days anymore, 5 days a week, but he finds purpose in the time he does work and it keeps his mind active.

Again, I suggest you should not retire until you consider all of the ramifications of retirement. Consider not only the numbers and financial aspects but your expenses and where and how you would like to spend your retirement. Oddly enough many new retirees in the first six months to a year find themselves spending more and they can't understand it.

Simply, they have more time to do more things – spend time with family, maybe travel, go to the movies, pursue hobbies, dine out. And many find themselves busier than ever pursuing those dreams they weren't able to while not retired. From conversations with my clients it seems that after about a year or so of retirement they had developed a better sense of balance and were better able to enjoy retirement.

Still able to pursue hobbies and interests but balanced with activities, sometimes compensated employment, that keeps them engaged with a sense of purpose.

In retirement, we should try to live abundantly. We've worked hard; we've saved for this time. Remember your early retirement years is probably the time you want to travel, when your knees don't ache as much and your hips won't hurt as much. When you're in your late 70's to mid 80's traveling may be a little more demanding. So consider as you plan to or actually retire what activities you would like to do and when may be more feasible – either because of expense or potential physical limitations.

PART ONE: MAY I RETIRE PLEASE?

Retirement, n.: An elusive goal that many strive to achieve. While past retirees had an easier time in planning for that goal, those of us today have found that retiring when and how we want to, is becoming more and more challenging.

While the retirement age used to begin for those 40+, today, most retire at about 65. This book will help guide you not only in preparing NOW for your future of non-working bliss, but also how to keep yourself there once you ARE retired. If you're anything like most people on the brink of retirement today, you're already asking yourself whether or not you're ready for retirement. When I say ready, I mean financially of course. You could very well have enough money to retire *now* but don't realize it yet. On the other hand, you may be ready for retirement but come to the conclusion that you don't have enough money yet, or aren't sure how much money you *do* need to be able to retire comfortably. Either way, this book will help you determine where you are in life, how you can prepare for your retirement, and what measures you can take to ensure that you are secured financially and prepared mentally for the big transition!

But always remember, in order for your retirement to be a successful one, you need to balance your income, expenses and assets. This is the most essential part so let me say it again: <u>To retire successfully, you need to balance your income, expenses and assets</u>.

DO I HAVE WHAT I NEED TO MEET MY MAIN GOALS?

DEALING WITH DEBT

Debts are something nobody wants, yet is impossible not to incur them. People with lower incomes tend to have a harder time staying away from debt accumulation because no matter what, they need basic human necessities such as food, clothes, and a roof over their heads.

However, people with higher incomes are able to not only comfortably be able to afford those basic human needs, but as the saying goes: the money is burning holes in their pockets. They have it and they figure that they may as well spend it, thus creating debt. No matter which economic class you are closer to, both can bring down their level of debt.

WHAT DO I DO NOW TO BRING DOWN MY DEBT

Pre-Retirement:

By reducing or eliminating debt, you can help save for when you're older and ready to tell the world where it can go. Budgeting is a proven way to help manage, reduce, and eventually eliminate debt. Start by drafting a list of your monthly income for both yourself and your spouse (if married).

Below, you will find Kat and her husband, John's budget sheet:

Total Income:	$7831.18
Net (Kat's) $5,833	70,000 ÷ 12 = 5,833
Net (John's) $3,750	45,000 ÷ 12 = 3,750
Gross (Kat's) $4,569	5,833 x 21.68% = 1,264 5,833 – 1,264 = 4,569
Gross (John's) $2,937	3,750 x 21.68% = 813 3,750 – 813 = 2,937
Government Benefits $125.18	Armed Forces Tax Benefits $125.18
Other Income $200.00	Independent Cosmetic Sales $200.00

Now that you have a clear figure of how much you make in a month, you need to list both your Fixed and your Variable expenses. Fixed expenses would be the mortgage or the car loan while a Variable expense would be the non-fat mocha latte – or five – that you have each day.

Kat and John's fixed expenses don't surpass their total monthly income. (See next page).

Fixed Expenses	Total Fixed Expenses: $1280.00
Mortgage	$500.00
Hydro	$150.00
Gas & Water Heating	$150.00
House Insurance	$120.00
Car Payment	$150.00
Car Insurance	$150.00
Cable/Satellite	$80.00
Telephone	$40.00
Cell Phone	$100.00
Internet	$120.00
Health Insurance	$50.00
Life Insurance	$50.00

However, their variable expenses (seen on the pages below) are leaving them with little left to save for retirement.

Variable Expenses	Total Variable Expenses: $5830.00
Allowances	$1000.00
Car Fuel	$600.00
Car Maintenance	$80.00
Public Transit	$0.00
Tolls/Taxi's/Parking	$2,400
Medical/Dental	$200.00
Groceries/Clothes	$400.00
Pets	$75.00
Family/Gifts	$150.00
Vacation	$0.00
Charities	$100.00
Restaurants	$75.00
Entertainment	$100.00

Hobbies/Sports	$50.00	
Clubs/Unions	$150.00	
Bank Fees	$50.00	
Emergency Fund	$100.00	
Savings	$250.00	
Debt Repayments	$500.00	
Total Expenses:	**Total Income:**	**Left Over:**
$7,681.00	**$7,831.18**	**$150.18**

Looking over Kat and John's budget sheet, anything highlighted in green is an uncontrollable number. You can't change them no matter how long you try and Jedi Mind Trick the people in charge. However, the other colors, especially the numbers in orange, **can** be changed. There is no reason why those numbers cannot decrease and the savings then put towards your retirement portfolio. After all, which is more deserving, eating out 5 times a week now or saving some of that so that you can retire more comfortably?

Find a compromise with your budget. Instead of buying that latte every day, have one on Friday to celebrate the end of the workweek; and instead of going to the movies every weekend, have a movie night at home with a film rented from the public library – it's free!

Now, before you go all crazy dumping the money you've just saved into your portfolio – stop! Remember the very end of the list with that lovely heading of DEBT? Start repaying your debts *first,* before going crazy trying to save money for later. That's not to say you shouldn't put anything away yet, but just to do so in moderation until your debts are erased.

Do you owe the government? Pay them. Do you still owe car payments? Pay them. Do you owe the credit card company? For the sake of your sanity, pay them before they call you at all hours of the night.

Lastly, do you owe family members and relatives? If you do, don't just pay them what you owe, give them a bit extra. Why? Because they were likely trying to save for their own retirement and your borrowing put a speed-bump in the way.

After Retirement:

If you are retired but are struggling to stay that way, all is not lost. Like with those who are planning for their retirement, making and adhering to a budget AFTER can help you stay retired comfortably.

Unlike the Pre-Retirement budget sheet, there are now options to consider when looking things over. If you're paying a mortgage on a large house but do not intend to spend as much time living in it, or there's no longer a need to own something so large, then it may be time to consider moving.

Yes, moving does cost money, but depending on the value of the property you are sitting on and what you require for a new home, it may not be as costly to do; especially if you arrange to move your pre-existing mortgage right along with you.

'Can I Move My Mortgage?'

Yes, you can. It may be the best thing to do considering that the interest rate on your existing mortgage won't inflate as many of us have fixed mortgages. Purchasing a new home and then getting a new mortgage would subject you to the increased rates that those of us buying homes now are sighing over.

However, there is one small (or big, depending on how you look at it) drawback when doing this: you will incur penalties when you pack your mortgage *with your furniture*.

Nevertheless, it can save you money in the long run as most retirees will not move again. Make sure you discuss this option in detail with a financial planner before going ahead with it. You want to be absolutely certain that you are saving money, even after the penalties, and that the interest rate on a new mortgage would not be lower than the one you own already.

If the mortgage you bought back in 1988 was $250,000 at an interest rate of 3.95% amortized over 25 years, then this is what you should be paying in monthly payments:

$$M=P[(1+i)^n]\div[(1+i)^n-1]$$

M = Monthly payment   i = Interest   n = Number of Payments

To calculate i: $0.0395\div12=0.003291$

To calculate n: $12\times25=300$

So now the formula looks like this:

$$M=P[(1.003291)^{300}]\div[(1+i)^{300}-1]$$

Now, before you ask me where the '1' in front of .003291 is, remember the equation was (1+i) so just add a one in front of the decimal point.

The next step is to solve for $(1+i)^n$:

$(1.003291)^{300}=3.34430$

Which changes our formula to:

$$M=P[(0.003291\times3.34430)\div(3.344310-1)]$$

Totaling: 0.00496

So now

$$M=250,000\times0.00496=\$1,172.50$$

Your monthly payments should be $1,172.50 if you intend to pay off your mortgage in 25 years. If the proposed new payments are higher than the amount you calculate, you are better off packing it up with that vase your mother-in-law gave you.

Another key point to remember is that the interest rates you pay on your mortgage are deductable from your yearly tax returns. If you want to know how much in interest you can claim for, or your accountant should be claiming for you:

$$I=(M \times N)-A-P$$

I = Interest   M = Monthly Payments
N = Number of Payments   A = Amount of the Mortgage
P = Principle

Using the previously calculated example with no:
    I=(1,172.50x300)=351,750
    351,750-250,000=101,750

    101,750-250,000=148,250

    I= $148,250

Your principle number depends on the amount you've paid off for your mortgage. In this example, it's only the first year and so the principle amount of $250,000 doesn't change. The more you pay off, the less you have to claim on your taxes, but the sooner you know you'll own your home.

This now leads us to the age-old question of whether or not you should've paid off your mortgage before retiring. The problem is that you can ask your financial advisor and they'll give you one answer and if you ask another for a second opinion.... well, you see what I'm getting at.

If you intend to downsize your home and your mortgage is already paid off, then unfortunately, it likely means getting stuck with another one. The amount of the mortgage depends solely on what the equity of the home you live in now is worth.

If the equity outweighs the price of your new home, then you could get away with not having a new mortgage, but in most situations, this is not the case.

If you are, however, close to paying off the mortgage because you wanted to own your home, consider slowing or decreasing the payments just long enough to pack it with you when you move.

Own More Than One Vehicle?

When looking over your budget sheet consider how many cars you own, their make, model, fuel efficiency and how much driving about you intend to do after you're retired.

The fact is, most retirees can get by owning just one vehicle. Without the hassle of going to work day in and day out, the need for more than one car lessens; especially as time goes on.

Selling off any other vehicles or updating the one you already own to a pre-used fuel efficient model can save you from pricy insurance rates, the rising cost of gas and leave you a bit more money in your portfolios.

Pre- and Post-Retirement Saving Ideas:

Accurate Expenses?

Many of us don't check our shopping bills for accuracy, especially if the item is small and inconsequential, but it is important to remember to check not only your grocery bills, but any home renovation bills as well. Make sure that any and all charges are correct, including your credit card statements. Banks are famous for being less than forthcoming in wanting you to stop paying them money that you owe, either in interest or before the interest even accumulates. If something is wrong with any bill or statement you receive, make certain you get it fixed.

If you get any home repairs done, make certain to check the reliability of the company and maintenance worker. Do a quick background check, even if it costs some money to do it. Trust me, it will save you not only a large sum of money, but the hassle of needing to redo a job and repay someone else to do the job that should have been fixed the first time around.

Shop By Comparison

In olden days, we all knew where to go to buy our groceries. The butcher sold the meat, the baker sold the bread and the dairy farmer had the milk and cheese. Today, everything is accumulated into one place – even department stores or grocery stores are selling the opposite's items. It is important to check the prices of the items you need, especially if it's a big item purchase.

Check the flyers for your local stores and then make a list of the items you intend to buy there. By comparing the prices of your weekly shopping items, you can save money bit by bit that will add up in the long-run. This isn't called being stingy, it's called being smart with how you spend your money!

HOW DO I PLAN TO RETIRE ON ENOUGH TO LIVE ON?

Live Comfortably

If you plan to retire comfortably, whether that's in five years or ten, then you need to start number crunching now to see what you need in order to make that happen. The estimated amount of money you need after you retire is about 60-70% of the income you're already making now. (See Retirement-at-a-Glace worksheet near the end of this book). However, it also depends on whether or not you plan to travel after retirement, if so, then you'll need to factor in more money than originally thought of providing none of the following apply:

- You've paid off your mortgage

- Your children are financially independent

- You've eliminated your debts

- You will no longer be accumulating work-related expenses like commuting or eating out

- Social Security will replace 45% of your income due to being in the middle-class

You've created a budget sheet already to calculate your current living expenses, refer to it and ask yourself the following:

- Do I intend to travel after I retire?

Whether for pleasure or to see family if you want to travel once you're retired, you need to factor this into the income you're already making. This means that you need to factor it into your budget sheet in order to start saving for it now.

- Do I intent to relocate?

Many people choose to move in order to downsize their homes. If you do, keep in mind the possibilities of moving to a low-cost area where the price of living won't be as high. Not only will it save you money, but what you do save can be used in case of unforeseen expenses, such as…

- Medical Expenses?

If there is a history of disease or known medical conditions then there is a chance that something could happen to you. It is important to set aside money in case anything does happen. Medical bills are costly, but if you plan in advance for them, then the strain on your finances won't be AS horrifying.

Inflation

The next thing you need to plan for is that lovely cost of inflation. Every year, prices increase for daily things such as groceries and gas.

While no one can accurately predict what the inflation rate will be, you can estimate a possible percentage based off past inflation rates; and while no one wants to, estimate a HIGHER inflation rate then the ones from the year before. Unfortunately, that's just how money greedy the government is. The following will help you to predict the amount needed for when inflation occurs:

Using Microsoft Excel, open a new document and type in the following:

	A	B	C	D
1	Year	Retirement Income Needed		
2	2011	65000		
3	2012			
4	2013			
5	2014			
6	2015			
7	2016			
8	2017			
9	2018			
10	2019			
11	2020			

Next, we need to tell the computer to calculate the inflation rate for us using what is known as Formulas. In this case, our Formula to calculate 65,000x1.03 is written as =B2*1.03. The computer will automatically take the amount listed in B2 and multiply it by 1.03% as shown below:

	A	B	C	D
1	Year	Retirement Income Needed		
2	2011	65000		
3	2012	=B2*1.03		
4	2013			
5	2014			
6	2015			
7	2016			
8	2017			
9	2018			
10	2019			
11	2020			

The amount now listed in B3 will be slightly higher than that of B2; this is due to the inflation rate of 3%.

	A	B	C	D
1	Year	Retirement Income Needed		
2	2011	65000		
3	2012	66950		
4	2013			
5	2014			
6	2015			
7	2016			
8	2017			
9	2018			
10	2019			
11	2020			

Now, if you want to find out the amount of inflation for all the years listed, in this example ten, then take your mouse and click on the little black square of the bold black box currently outlining B3 and drag it down as far as your years go. Like such:

	A	B	C	D
1	Year	Retirement Income Needed		
2	2011	65000		
3	2012	66950		
4	2013			
5	2014			
6	2015			
7	2016			
8	2017			
9	2018			
10	2019			
11	2020			

Once you let go of the mouse button, the numbers that the computer calculated will appear automatically.

	A	B	C	D
1	Year	Retirement Income Needed		
2	2011	65000		
3	2012	66950		
4	2013	68958.5		
5	2014	71027.26		
6	2015	73158.07		
7	2016	75352.81		
8	2017	77613.4		
9	2018	79941.8		
10	2019	82340.06		
11	2020	84810.26		

You can play with the percentage of inflation depending on the current trends just to see how much you will need while retired. The estimations for inflations take into account the number of years you plan to be retired, generally about 25-30 years, so keep that in mind as well.

SERIOUSLY, HOW MUCH DO I NEED TO RETIRE?

Knowing how much you need to start saving now so that you can retire when you want to can be overwhelming. Someone at the age of 22 has more time to start saving then someone at the age of 55. Often times we get so caught up with trying to keep our heads above water that by the time the age you want to retire at starts looming over your shoulder, we've no idea how to go about it. The following are a few ways to determine how much you might need when you retire.

Retirement Worksheet

This worksheet has been designed to help you think and forecast an estimated amount of money you will need before you can retire. Keep in mind that you will still need to budget after retiring.

Kat and John's Retirement Worksheet can be found on the next few pages:

1. Estimate your living expenses (Factor in 70% of current expenses)	**$49,000**
2. Estimate retirement income using:	
a. Social Security	$42,000
b. Pension Plan	$20,000
c. 401K	$10,000
d. Other Income (ex. Investments)	$50,000
3. Total Estimated Income (Add lines a-d)	$122,000
4. Net (Subtract Line 3 from Line 1)	$73,000
5. Estimate retirement years (Life expectancy of 90 years)	25 years if retired by 65.
6. Estimate return rate on investments (7% ave. on a conservative portfolio)	5.5%
7. Average rate of inflation	3.50%
8. Net inflation; adjust rate of return (Subtract Line 7 from Line 6)	2%
9. Assume Return Factor (Please refer to Table A below)	19.52%
10. Retirement Goal by 65 (Multiply Line 9 by Line 4)	$14,249.60

Table A	
Years of Retirement	**Net Return Factors**
15	12.85
16	13.58
17	14.29
18	14.99
19	15.68
20	16.35
21	17.01
22	17.66
23	18.29
24	18.91
25	19.52
26	20.12
27	20.71
28	21.28
29	21.84
30	22.40

Now, if the Net amount listed in Line 4 is positive, then you have more income than expenses. If the Net is negative, then you have too many expenses and need to rethink your plans. Re-evaluate your budget or find a second job as another source of income.

WHAT SORT OF ASSISTANCE DO I NEED?

If you're sitting there reading this book and staring at the last chapter going: *'Are you crazy? I can't possibly manage that by myself!'* then I doubt you're alone. For many people, reducing debt can be a struggle, especially if you really want that latte. Although it comes down to one's perseverance, sometimes you need that less-than-gentle shove in the right direction.

Talking things over with a financial advisor can help decrease tension and anxiety. Many of us are not number people, we avoided them in high school and we continue to do so today. Telling your advisor where things are now and where you want things to be in the future will help them to determine specific paths for you to take now so that you're prepared later on in life; or help you stay on your path so that you can continue being retired in comfort.

Another thing you could possible do is have your friends and family members support you. Let them know what's going on so that they can help you stay on target. If you go shopping and want to buy a pair of shoes or you want to bet on a pool game, your friends can be there to support and remind you of your goals so that you can stay on target.

ARE WE ON THE SAME PAGE?

You and I may be on the same page, but there is someone else to consider when planning for your retirement - your spouse. While most people often feel they can handle all of the family budgeting and finances by themselves, the fact is that it is important that both of you are working on this *together*. Handcuff your significant other to the table if you have to or hide their golf clubs, just make sure that you both cooperate in planning for retirement.

When talking about retirement you want to make sure that money is not the only thing discussed. Share with each other what it is you want to be able to do; whether it's travel, play more golf, crochet or just read books all day, you want to be sure that you're both happy once your lazy-days come about. Once you can talk to your spouse about those things, then ease financial aspects into the conversation bit by bit and make sure to listen to each other. If you do happen to get into an argument then stop and take a breather for a few days to mull over what the other person is saying and then come back to the discussion again with an open mind.

Once you are both able to talk freely and calmly about what you want out of retirement, it's time to start planning. Refer to the budget created and the inflation charts to determine if you will be financially secure to accomplish what it is you wish to do. Certain things may have to be put on hold for a little while in order to be financially stable, but just remember to work as a team and support each other's goals.

As your finances stabilize, talk about investing in a financial advisor. They can help you find the middle ground between the goals you both and come up with a plan to help both of you.

HOW WILL MY RETIREMENT AFFECT MY RELATIONSHIP WITH FAMILY AND FRIENDS?

Normally in life after your children grow up and leave, you don't see them or their children as often as you'd like but once retirement comes about you have a chance to spend a lot more time with the one's you love. This becomes especially important if your family lives in another state or country that you spend more time with them now that the opportunity has presented itself. However, this doesn't mean that if the relationship has been strained with your children before now that it will magically repair itself, but it can give you a chance to sort things out a bit better in order to see your grandchildren on a more regular basis. You can also help them in their retirement planning so that they can become better prepared in the long run.

The relationship with your spouse will also change once you retire. Most couples spend maybe a few hours with each other but if you both retire about the same time that may mean seeing a lot more of one another.

Make certain that while you want to spend more time with each other than you aren't placing a strain on the other person's nerves and take breaks from each other's company. The more time you spend with someone the more likely you are to argue and bicker, so make certain that there are other interests and hobbies that you have that will help give you both the space that you need.

This leads us to the relations you have with your friends. While you may lose the friends you had at work, you still have those you've grown up with and have stood next to you through all the changes in your life. Those friends may or may not have yet retired but regardless your retirement still gives you an opportunity to spend a bit more time with them.

LIVING BETTER FOR LESS!

Since you're a few years off from retiring you should begin enhancing your savings by reducing your expenses, this way you can also lower the amount required after you retire. The less you need for your retirement income, the more you can save for the unexpected. Knowing by how much you can lower your living expenses all depends on your needs but you can reduce your expenses three different ways:

- ***Find a cheaper alternative to getting what you already need.*** This refers back to the section on comparison-shopping, as it's not just for food or clothing, it relates to car insurance, travel, vehicles, and gasoline as well. If you can get what you require for a lower price than your retirement income will be lower than what has been estimated thus far.

- ***Eliminate debts and unnecessary expenses.*** As already discussed, it is important to reduce your debts as far down as they can go and cut costs on expenses that are not needed. What counts as an unnecessary expense all depends on the person. Most people like to drink beer or wine but that doesn't mean you have to drink the most expensive bottle out there. Find a cheaper made beverage that still tastes just as good and save what's left over for other, more important things.

- ***Move to where the cost of living is cheaper.*** Moving from a big city is an expense in and of itself, especially if you rely on public transportation. However, it can end up costing you more to live there than in the boonies, especially since the cost of homes in smaller places is nowhere near as high as they are in the city. This is because there are more people per square inch living in cities than there are living in towns or the boons. There's a reason people prefer living in Brooklyn and commuting to New York City each day, and it's not because they love the hassle of public transit.

Living on a modest income as a retiree is doable. The average amount recorded as of late that those retired are living off of is about $25,000 a year, which is 50% less than the normal family living on an estimated $47,000 per year. The problem is that those of heading into the luxury of retirement are living in a much different economy that your grandparents or even your own parents. The recession has made things more challenging for all, thus why even those who had planned for contingencies had to find a way to increase their retirement income and some had to go back to working for a while before things settled back down.

Although not intending to frighten anyone when I say this, the fact of the matter is that the economy is still not yet fully recovered from the recession and another one is a possibility in the future. That is why it is important to try and live off of as little as you actually need right now and plan for the possibility of needing more after you retire than originally thought of. You're retirement budget should be realistic and factor in any possible contingencies from needing long-term medical care, to being pulled back into an economic slump.

PART TWO: PERSONAL FINANCIAL PLAN

Your budget is under control, your debts are reduced and you are finally able to see an increase in money to be invested into your future. But how do you go about doing it? Knowing you need a Retirement Portfolio is one thing, but building it is another. It is important to remember to diversify your portfolio just in case something happens; like the Stock Markets crash. Keep an open mind about all options when deciding where to invest your hard-earned money.

WILL MY RETIREMENT PLAN PROVIDE ME WITH INCOME FOR LIFE?

While it is unlikely that all retirement plans will provide you with enough income for life, the more you start planning now, the better off you'll be in the future. Although your wish may be to retire at 65, if you delay it by another few years then you will be more financially secure once you are finally retired and it may be possible to live on the income planned.

ASSET ALLOCATION

An asset can be defined as something which can gain value over time or that can have collateral set against it. Typically assets are what you want to have plenty of instead of debts.

Assets can include cars, boats, jewelry, gold, real estate, stocks and bonds and trade tools. Now before you start debating that cars and boats are liabilities and not assets, as long as you own them without loans, they are indeed assets.

Unfortunately, even though your car and boat are assets, it is likely that they will be sold before you hit the age of retirement. When you do sell, get as good of a deal as you can get on them and invest the money elsewhere – providing you don't need another car.

Investing your assets in a conservative manner means that there is less risk in losing your money and while they are beneficial in a shorter span of time, no matter what you are still investing long-term even after you retire. It is important to consider all options when investing your money; even if the low-risk options seem better, they may not turnabout as much money as you need in the future.

The proper way to invest is to target the longevity of your money, meaning how long do you want your money to last you once you retire. You want what provides the best return with the least amount of risk over the period of your retirement of nearly 25-30 years. The longer you wait and the older you become before planning your retirement does shrink your time to invest BUT you should remember how long you intend to be alive after you retire and that your investments should last as long as your life does. Once you do retire, your 401K can be rolled over into another investment and continue to grow right along with your retirement.

PROJECTIONS AND FUTURE NEEDS

In planning for that elusive retirement there are a number of things that we can and cannot control, like the economy or whether or not the Mayan's have it right and we all die next year. Either way, do the best you can in attempting to plan for what you do and don't have control over. As we have already established a budget earlier on – yes I know I'm repetitive – we can move on to the next few things we can control.

Investing Regularly

Making regular investments as often as you can is important, even if it seems to be some menial amount of money, it can grow – especially if your investments gain interest over time. If you haven't started on your investments, be sure to do so the first possible moment you get.

Estate Planning

Everything you own is worth something, even after your death. It is important to allocate where you want things to go once that has happened to reduce the amount of debt to be placed on your family and loved ones. By writing your will, you can establish what you wish to do with material items and any investments still accumulating money. If you die without having written a will, the state claims possession of the items, including the house, any property you own, your bank accounts, material possessions, and investments. Make certain that if you do not want that to happen to write your will as soon as possible.

University/College Tuition

Tuition costs are on the rise and increase yearly. If you want to help your children or grandchildren financially then see about investing in an Education Savings Account or a Tax-Free Savings Account. Both will allow tax-free withdrawals for educational expenses for all levels of schooling you want available to your child/grandchild.

You may also consider looking into prepaid tuition and college plans that allow you to make higher contributions and withdrawals for increased expenses.

Now that you are prepared for some of the other issues that you can budget and save for, it is time to see what you can't plan for accurately.

7 THINGS YOU CANNOT PREDICT

<u>#1 Social Security</u>

While you pay into your Social Security account every month in preparation to receive the money back from the government, the fact is that it is highly unlikely that what you have paid into the account is what you'll be getting out of it.

The government is in so much debt themselves that they are taking the money that you pay them now and using it elsewhere for the time being. The fact of the matter is that on your Social Security statement they actually asterisk the amount that you're expecting and telling you that it is just not going to happen; but keep paying us anyways.

#2 Rate of Return

Trying to figure out which percentage to invest in as your rate of return is like picking which cup the pea is hiding under. Regardless of how much you estimate and what you choose as your return rate, the allocations of your assets will affect that rate and so you still won't actually know what it is you're getting.

#3 Inflation

That lovely thing I mentioned about preparing for earlier in this book is still not going to be something that is easily predicted. Currently everything from gasoline to food to clothes and public transit is on the rise due to inflation, but the fact remains that no one can predict how high it will be in 30 years.

#4 Retirement Age

If you're laughing then I'm guessing that you think you can actually retire at the age you want to. The issue is that while you want to be retired at that age it may not be possible, not because you don't have enough money, but because you might love working way too much to stop at some random age or you may be ill and have to come up with more money to pay off the bills. The fact is, while we may know when we want to retire the actual age we retire at can't be predicted.

#5 Activity During Retirement

No one knows what he or she'll be doing once they actually do retire. Some retirees become antsy after being idle for about a month and want to start working part-time just to do something with themselves. Once that happens what your planned income for retirement may change, especially if it requires commuting daily.

#6 Future Income

What someone makes now may not be what he or she makes in 5 years. They might be making more or they could be making less depending on their situation; they may've gotten laid off their old job or they may've gotten promoted. Your future income can impact your retirement planning significantly.

#7 End Of The World As We Know It

Stop giving me a 'you're nuts' look; you know nothing lasts forever. Whether something does happen next year that kills us all or we end up in another recession or even a third World War, the world we live in would ultimately change no matter what. We can't predict or stop it, only try and prepare as best we can for it.

IRA'S STOCKS, AND OTHER INVESTMENTS TOWARDS THE FUTURE

An IRA or Individual Retirement Account is a retirement plan that provides tax advantages for those saving for their retirements. An IRA may be the only investment in the stock market that you own. The problem is that too many go through all the trouble to start their retirement IRA's and then just sit idle waiting for them to mature. What you should be doing is making sure that you get a proper and fair return on your IRA's. A few brokers will allow you to spread your IRA's into other investments if the one's you are dealing with already do not.

Double or Nothing

How long it will take to double what you have invested can be calculated using the Rule of 72. Divide 72 by your annual return percentage and you'll get the number of years, with compound interest; it will take in order to double down. For example if you make a 5% investment per year it'll take 14.4 years to double your money. If you want to earn more, faster, invest in a higher percentage each year on your IRA's.

Compound It Down

Compounding the interest on the percentage you invest in your IRA's each month earns you money. If you start with $5,000 in your IRA, earning 5% each month, then in 20 years:

$$A=P(1+r/n)nt$$

A= Final Amount   n= Number of times compounded per year

P= Principal Amount Initially Invested

r= Annual Interest Rate (decimal)   t= Years

Plugging in what we know our formula becomes:

$$A= 5000(1+.116/12)12x20$$

Now calculate (1+.116/12) and 12x20; plug the new numbers into the formula:

$$A=5000(1.0096)240$$

Multiply the Principal by the interest rate:

$$A=5000x1.0096 = 5048$$

Finally:

$$A=5048x240 = 1,211,520$$

This means that in 20 years the amount now invested in your IRA is $1,211,520.00. This amount is based off a 5%/month interest rate compounded each month over a course of 20 years. Depending on the percentage and the number of times per year that you compound that rate, the number will be different.

Stocks

Stocks are the route most people take when investing in their retirements. Because certain stocks continuously rise with the market, the value of the holder's investment rises as well.

However, playing the markets is a risky thing to do, especially if you're uncertain which companies to buy shares in.

Research which companies you want to buy shares in and keep a watch on their daily gains and losses for about a month before making a decision. You may find that while some companies start off well, they can quickly go under. Long-lasting companies such as Microsoft, HP, Toshiba, Chevrolet, GMC, DOW and NASDAQ are good options to choose from when buying shares.

How much you should invest in stocks is said to be determined by your age based on a 100-year life expectancy. If you're 25, then 75% of your investments should be put away into various stocks; and if you're 65, then 35% should be put into stocks. Regardless, do what you think is best for you and your nesting egg.

Bonds

While U.S. Savings Bonds have been faded out by the U.S. Treasury, they still issue bonds which offer non-marketable securities. Meaning that unlike with stocks, they don't depend on the market in order to mature.

- Series EE Bonds: These bonds are issued at 50% their face value and reach maturity in thirty years, but can reach face value in seventeen. Interest is added monthly and paid upon the time the holder cashes in.
- Series I Bonds: These bonds are issued at face value and have a variable yield based on inflation. The interest rate on this bond depends on the buyer. If they buy it with a fixed interest rate, it will remain constant for the life of the bond. If they purchase a variable rate, the interest is reset every six months.

Gold

Gold is a limited resource that's value fluctuates along with the markets. Gold is exchanged at a rate of its potential value and not its actual one. Unless all the gold in the world is excavated, it is hard to give an accurate value to gold. However, because it is a limited resource, its value skyrockets more than it drops. Investing in the gold exchange can be costly at first, but will pay off faster than bonds.

However, you do not need to have stocks in the gold exchange in order to make money from it. If you have gold you can sell it at a percentage of its market value. Keep tabs on the market and then when you decide to sell, make sure you are getting your money's worth.

Jewelry

How many of us have accumulated an endless supply of watches, earring, bracelets, rings and necklaces? Likely, all of us at one point or another buy a piece or are given a piece of jewelry that's now collecting dust elsewhere.

While most items are not as valuable because of their components, others can be sold for cash that can be invested elsewhere. Make certain that the person you are selling your treasured items to is a reputable dealer that gives you the items true worth. When in doubt, consult more than one expert just so you feel more confident in your decision to sell.

Timeshares

While some may know exactly what timeshares are, many of you may not. A time share is like a stock. You buy a share of the company, but instead of watching the markets, it's like owning a piece of real estate. You own the rights to a piece and time of property. Each year you can either use your time at a location specified, or you can bank them and roll it over onto another year.

What one may not know is that timeshares can be upgraded, gifted and sold. If you own timesharing and are not planning on using it or have not used it in a while, you may consider selling it and investing the money elsewhere. Timeshares are sold at face value as the value doesn't increase over time like with stocks, bonds, gold, jewelry or coins.

OTHER PLANNING CONSIDERATIONS

Health Insurance is something to be considered when planning for your retirement. As you become older, your become more susceptible to medical issues, especially if there's a history of problems in your family and any unforeseen medical expenses can easily place you into debt and force you out of retirement in order to pay them off.

Many people have health coverage through their work, but once you retire you will lose any coverage you have so it is important to find a health insurance company that will provide you with what you require at a price that is affordable to pay each month and still allow you to be retired. Finding a health care provider that is right for you may require hours of comparing different companies that will provide you with the coverage you need, the coverage you can afford and whether or not you can afford to pay for what is not covered should something unexpected arise.

Find out if they cover any current prescriptions or if you'll need to consider upgrading from the plan you have in mind to a different one in order for your prescriptions to be covered.

Once you have decided on a health program that suits your needs, you'll need to enroll as soon as possible before you're work coverage expires. Some companies may require you to fill out medical history questionnaires to weigh the risks of having you as a client. If you're concerned or are denied, look into companies that don't require you to take a medical questionnaire. After everything has been cleared and your new health coverage has kicked in, then you can retire from work with ease knowing that no matter what you still have a safety net beneath your feet should you need it.

PRIORITIES WHEN PLANNING

WHAT IF... EXPENSES GO UP

Due to an annual inflation rate, expenses are liable to go up while you are retired. Work-related, home maintenance and income taxes will decrease once you are retired, but things like travel, healthcare and recreational activities will increase in expense. These can't be helped as many retirees intend to travel and be active until their later years in life. However, because you know that these expenses will be increasing, plan ahead for them. Because there are three stages of retirement, Early, Mid and Late, it is important to try and prepare for all three. Use the table below as a guideline for planning your expenses during all three stages of retirement, and make sure to discuss it with your spouse as well, just so you know how much to start saving for.

Ken Mahoney - http://www.thesmartinvestors.com

	Current Expenses	Expenses During Retirement		
		Early	Mid	Late
Shelter				
Rent or mortgage payments				
Real estate taxes				
Insurance				
Household Operation				
Home repair, yard care				
Water, heat, electricity				
Telephone, cable, Internet				
Waste disposal				
Household supplies				
Other				
Home Improvement & Upkeep				
Furniture, fixtures				
Floor coverings				
Kitchen equipment				
Yard equipment, supplies				
Automobile & Transportation				
Car payments				
Repairs				
Gasoline and oil				
License, registration				
Insurance				
Medical, Health				
Medications				
Physician, dentist visits				
Eyeglasses, hearing aids				
Health insurance				
Long-term care insurance				
Life insurance				
Taxes				
Federal income tax				
State income tax				
Food, Beverages				
Food at home				
Food away from home				
Entertaining expenses				
Clothing				
New clothing				
Dry cleaning/laundry service				
Shoe repair				
Personal				
Barber/beauty shops				
Toiletries, cosmetics				
Stationery, postage				
Recreation, Education, Other				
Books, subscriptions				
Club memberships, dues				
Movies, concerts, sports events				
Hobby supplies				
Vacations, travel, celebrations				
Adult continuing education				
Pets: care, food, license				
Contributions				
Gifts				
Other				
Savings, Investments				
Monthly totals: (if monthy figures entred)				
Yearly Totals:				

WHAT IF... MY HEALTH GIVES OUT

There are few things in life we can actually prepare ourselves for and unfortunately, health issues are not always something that can be planned out, not matter how hard we try. If you know of a pre-existing condition then planning becomes a bit easier, but there are many health issues that can arise without having a pre-existing condition.

Having health care can help you be prepared for some of the unexpected medical costs that can incur but so can buying a long-term health policy in case of something like Alzheimer's. A long-term policy can be bought as an individual or as a group depending on your needs, be sure to shop around so that you are still financially protected after your purchase the policy.

However, buying into a policy all depends on your family situation. If your family is dealing with their own debts or they live a long ways away from you then it may be a good idea to consider long-term care.

Your family, as devoted to you as they are, will only be able to endure caring for you for so long before the stress takes its toll on them and their health as well.

WHAT IF… I WANT TO TRAVEL THE WORLD

It's not uncommon for retirees to want to travel during their early retirement. The important thing to remember is that it should be planned out prior to retiring in order to make it financially feasible. Knowing where you intend to travel and for how long will determine how much needs to be saved beforehand. If it's to visit family that's out of state then the costs will likely include two-way air-fare and a small amount for spending as many who visit with their families stay with them during their visit.

If, however, the trip is elsewhere that needs to include hotel, food, touring and spending allowances then the amount needed to be save will be quite a bit more.

When booking your trip, try and get an all-inclusive package to help make things a bit more affordable and don't forget to add travel insurance as well in case someone falls ill or your money or bags are stolen.

PART THREE: YOUR HEALTH & WELL-BEING...DURING RETIREMENT YEARS

Once you've retired your health becomes a main factor in how long you will live enjoying those days. It is important to keep active and maintain a well-balanced diet that suits your particular needs. During your early years of retirement and into the middle years, you should stay fit by taking up a new sport or increasing your involvement in an old one. Some of the best ways to keep fit as you get older are yoga, walking and swimming as you can control how much you exert yourself. Be sure to listen to your body, it's knows you better than even a doctor.

AM I READY FOR THE COST OF LONG-TERM CARE IN THE EVENT THAT I NEED IT?

As previously mentioned, having a long-term health care plan in the event that something happens to you can expensive. Some policies may have a waiting period of 30 days or more depending on if it's at home or at facility care. During that time period you'll have to pay the deductible out of pocket before the rest of your care is covered by the policy.

Since the amount all depends on the plan, try to find out what the deductible is and start saving for it as soon as you can so as to not incur debt instead. Also, your premium on your policy won't be waived until after you've been in care for the required number of days, which means, not only are you paying the deductible, but the premium out of pocket as well.

To collect under your policy, you insurance company will decide if you are unable to perform daily functions like eating, getting dressed, bathing, administering medication, moving, and going to the washroom. They will consult with the doctors and care-givers in order to determine whether or not you can be paid out, however, your policy may allow you to have your own doctor determine that fact free of charge. Another thing to consider is that your rates may increase depending on the company and who else has purchased the plan at the age you did.

How much your plan will actually cost you depends on a variety of factors: age, health, location, and the features you want in your policy. Ultimately though, the price will depend on the cost of long-term care across the country. This is because long-term care is no different than insurance on homes or cars; the price is reflected by the over-all increase or decrease in cost across the country and while your premiums may not increase severely, they may include an inflation clause that will increase the coverage each year without increasing the premium.

HOW WILL I SPEND MY RETIREMENT YEARS?

Filling Time

Without the structure of the office environment to dutifully report to five days a week, week after week, month after month, and year after year, you're going to have a lot of free time on your hands. A lot of time—time not automatically scheduled for a department meeting. Time not scheduled so tight that you only have five minutes to eat lunch, so it has to be at your desk and without time for digesting before you have to go to yet another client meeting. Now you can finally *choose* how you spend your time. Fear may have just struck you if you don't already have a plan as to how you're going to spend your retirement years. If you haven't already made a plan, now is the time to start thinking about what you're going to choose to do with all of your newfound time. Maybe you need a few ideas to get you started on the right track.

How Can I Spend My Time?

After years of your life wiled away working, you may need to take some time when you first retire just to unwind. Lying around in your pajamas reading books that have gone unread and watching movies and TV shows you haven't had time for in years. This kind of activity may suffice for a week or two but after that you may start looking for a more meaningful way to spend your time.

Many new retirees find themselves in a state of depression if they don't find a meaningful way to spend their time. After years of having a purpose, retirement makes them to start to feel worthless. This is especially true for the movers and shakers of the baby boom generation—a generation that has been on full-throttle since day one and has no interest in letting retirement slow them down now.

New career

You have worked for thirty years or so at a job that you had out of necessity not want. You had to pay the bills and cover family expenses and your career job allowed you to own up to your responsibilities. But maybe it wasn't the career of your dreams. Maybe it was, but more often than not, it wasn't. Well, now is your chance.

In retirement, you have the time and the drive to start a new career. Maybe you want to work in an industry that relates to your college degree. Maybe it's a totally new undertaking that you have zero experience in. Whatever your dream job is, find it and pursue it.

Start a business

After working for the man (or the woman) for all of those years, now you can work for yourself. Be your own boss. Many people retire from working for a company, but choose to turn their experience and knowledge into a business of their own.

Some retirees even become consultants for the company they retired from in the first place.

Maybe you don't want to continue in the same line of work, but prefer to branch out in a new a career and launch your own business while doing it. Check into your state laws on how to start various types of businesses—LLCs, partnerships, sole proprietorships or corporations—and the kind of licensing you may need to run the business. You can also consider buying and opening a franchise.

Franchises already have the licensing, rules, regulations, marketing, strategies, and plans figured out for you. Many franchise opportunities offer financing so you don't have to deplete your savings or sell investments to come up with the money to start it. If you think buying a franchise is for you, contact the corporate headquarters of the franchise you are interested in opening or check out some of your options on www.franchisegator.com.

Whether you choose to start your own business from scratch or decide to buy and run a franchise, you can continue to work in retirement for yourself—being your own boss and still creating income.

Volunteer

If you prefer to do something meaningful with your time, but don't need or want to be paid for doing them, consider volunteering. Every community in the country has numerous volunteer opportunities available.

Volunteering is a double fulfilling prophecy because it makes you feel good to help someone in need or to contribute to a cause you feel strongly about, and it provides help to those in need or contributes to furthering the cause you are volunteering for.

You can find volunteer opportunities by calling local organizations, charities, schools, hospitals, or churches to find out what type of volunteer opportunities are available.

There are also websites where you can get information on volunteer opportunities in your area. These websites can also match you up with volunteer opportunities based on your location and interests. Visit sites like www.volunteermatch.org, www.volunteersolutions.org, and www.volunteer.gov for more information on finding a volunteer opportunity near you.

Travel

Having the time to travel is what many retirees look forward to during retirement. How much you can travel depends on your personal financial situation, but many find a way of traveling full-time—even selling their home and buying an RV to travel the country. Pull out your passport and dust it off. Take that trip to Europe you've always wanted to take but never had the time to do. Or load up the car and drive across country like you and your spouse have always talked about doing. Just hit the open road (or sky) and see what the world has to offer.

Leisure activities

We all have activities that we enjoy doing in our spare time. Now that you have more spare time, you have more time to spend doing your leisure activities. Golfing and playing tennis for the sports enthusiasts; hiking trails, camping and gardening for the naturalists; and reading and writing for the creative. Whatever way you enjoy spending your time, now is the time to enjoy even more hours doing it.

Craft/Hobby

For all you crafty people reading this, your retirement can become full-time arts and crafts time. Making handmade greeting cards, sewing, knitting, scrapbooking, building model trains, planes or automobiles—whatever your craft or hobby pleasure, now you can spend more of your time doing what you love.

Part-time employment

Maybe you still need to earn a little money on top of your retirement income, or you just want to work out of the home for a few hours a day or a couple days a week. Consider taking on a part-time job. Working part-time is another way of getting to work in a new industry or even in your old industry without having to devote a full-time schedule doing it.

It helps to keep you active, allows you to exercise your brain, and gives you a little extra spending money. And some part-time jobs—like Starbucks' baristas—not only receive part-time pay, but employee benefits as well. Working may mean more to you than the pay if you need healthcare or retirement benefits.

Find balance in your life

Retirement doesn't have to mean full-time devotion to any one activity. It is a time for you to find life balance. A time for you to spend time doing what you enjoy—finding balance in your life between what you enjoy doing and taking care of your responsibilities at the same time. And it may be that one of the activities listed above or some combination of these activities help you to achieve this balance.

HEALTHY LIFESTYLE CHOICES

Enjoying your retirement years to its fullest is not just about having enough money to cover your living expenses either. Your retirement will be more enjoyable if your mind and body are in good health. Keeping your mind and body active, spending time with people you care about, and doing things you enjoy all contribute to a retirement worth living.

As a boomer, you're expected to live longer than any generation before you, which means there are things you have to take into consideration about your health that no other generations had to think about. Just like any situation there are good and bad things associated with being part of a generation that has a longer life span.

Being part of the "Viagra Generation" may mean that you can have more fun than your parents did, but you also face more risks. And you're retiring in an age when preventive care and healthy living can keep you going for decades longer than many of your ancestors.

Research has shown that both exercise and social contact contribute to longevity and can significantly improve your quality of life. So take a walk, or better yet, organize a walking club. Volunteer for causes for which you have a passion. Start a small business. Challenge yourself by learning something you've always been curious about, whether it's origami or flying down the slopes on a snowboard with the grandkids. Disconnect the tube and curl up with a good book or spend hours chatting with a friend. Retirement is about being healthy in your mind and in your body--spending time with those you've been too busy to fully enjoy in the past.

A Healthy Mind

Research shows that as you age, it is important to keep your mind active. By stimulating your brain and keeping it moving and thinking, it helps your mind and body in shape. Exercising your mind can be accomplished in many ways. You have to choose the ways you enjoy the most. Reading, doing crossword puzzles or Sodoku puzzles are just a few of the ways you can keep your brain thinking and working—exercising the most important part of your body.

Staying active with a part-time or full-time job is another way that researchers have found that active retirees stay healthy. It may be partially psychological, since working provides a sense of worth, but using your brain to complete your daily work activities stimulates your thinking and knowledge skills, which helps to keep your brain active.

A Healthy Body

Let's say you spent your high school and college years actively playing team sports. Your college and adult life were spent on the tennis and racquetball courts, but now that your body is aging, it may prove to be more difficult for you to participate in the activities you once did. This doesn't mean you have to give up your exercise or sports activities. It just means you may need to trade in one form of exercise for another. Try something new. Open your mind to an activity you may have not otherwise even considered trying. It's amazing what affect it can have on how you feel, how you look and how you age gracefully.

For example, yoga is seeing the most growth in popularity among seniors age 55 and older—even reaching into those in their 80s. Many seniors are finding the calming affects of yoga something that provides nurturing to both their minds and their bodies.

It is one form of exercise that many are finding beneficial to get them through the tough times of retirement—financial stress, family stress, illnesses and diseases and more. For many, it creates positive thinking, which goes back to envisioning yourself into a successful retirement like we discussed earlier in the book.

Start or join an exercise group

Exercising with someone else is always more fun than doing it alone. Having an exercise partner or group is also motivating. When you don't feel like exercising your partner or group will motivate you to take that walk, do the yoga class or hit the tennis court. And vice versa, when your partner or someone in your group doesn't feel like exercising, you can motivate them to get up and go. Start or join an exercise group in your area. It may focus on a particular activity like walking or tennis or maybe it's a group that varies its activities each time it meets—canoeing one week, walking a mile the following week, and hiking a nature trail the week after that.

Eating healthy

Most think that eating healthy involves giving up all of the wonderful foods you enjoy eating. This, however, is not the case. Easting healthy is about substituting good ingredients for the bad ingredients, when and where you can. For example, instead of using vegetable oil to bake your favorite cake, substitute plain yogurt instead. It means baking chicken instead of frying it. It means finding alternative ways to make your favorite yummies. There are many websites and cookbooks that provide light cooking alternatives for most of your favorite meals. These resources also offer proper substitutes to make your recipes healthier without sacrificing the taste. Cooking Light.com and its series of online recipes and hardcover cookbooks is just one example of a resource you can turn to for healthier recipe choices.

Take a cooking class

Many community colleges or community centers offer healthy cooking classes. Registering for and completing a cooking course is a fun way to challenge yourself and introduce yourself to a healthier way of cooking and eating. Join with your spouse, a friend, or even a group of friends to heighten the fun of taking the classes. It's a productive way of spending your time in retirement because it keeps your mind active—you're learning—and it also helps to create a healthier body.

Start or join a cooking club

There are also cooking clubs specifically geared toward older individuals. Cooking clubs not only provide you with information on creating a healthy diet for your age group, but many cooking clubs share food. This means that the class is sectioned off into groups and each group is assigned a particular meal or meal course. Once the meal or course is made, it is packaged up for each group member to take home to eat or freeze for thawing a reheating later.

Check your local newspapers, community centers, and online groups for groups or clubs in your area. If you don't find any, consider starting a cooking club or group yourself.

Medication

We have more medication now than we have ever had. While your mom may have taken blood pressure medication, there are now ten blood pressure medications for your doctor to prescribe for your high blood pressure. And with all of these new medications come a whole new set of side effects. Side effects that you need to be aware of for each medication you are taking because these side effects can cause you to have to take even more medication—working like a domino effect.

For this reason, alternative medicine and natural supplements have increased in popularity. It's not just the young jock trying to buff up for his wrestling team that is hitting the natural health store to buy up vitamins and health supplements. Where our healthy eating and exercise routines may fall short, vitamins and natural supplements can fulfill the needs our body has as we get older. Talk with your doctor about the medications you are taking and what affects vitamins and supplements may have on you, but be open-minded to taking care of your health medically and naturally.

Regular checkups

While it is wise to have regular check-ups with your doctor at all ages of your life, it becomes increasingly important as you get older. Your susceptibility to illnesses and diseases increase as our body ages, so it is important to see your doctor regularly to monitor your health.

The quicker the doctor can detect medical problems or conditions, the better chances you have of controlling it or getting rid of it altogether.

ABUNDANCE THINKING

To a large extent, the sort of retirement you have will be determined by your outlook, as well as by the energy you put into creating the life you want.

Let's start with the outlook you have about your retirement. How do you view your retirement years? Do you see the glass as half-full or half-empty? People who see their glasses as half-full, tend to be positive thinkers. And positive thinkers tend to attract positive results. Their glasses keep filling up. Negative thoughts, on the other hand, tend to drain those glasses. In the end, those who think they can achieve a goal, whether financial, political, or social, are generally proven correct, while those who think they can't are similarly likely to be proven correct.

Abundance in your positive thinking proves the laws of attraction correct.

We've all been in uncomfortable situations with our minds racing, exaggerating likely outcomes, and raising our blood pressure. Those fantasies and fears that compulsively race through our minds need to be noted and consciously controlled. Otherwise, the fears take charge of our lives. This is especially true when planning for your retirement years. It is similar to a self-fulfilling prophecy. If you spend so much time worrying about the doom and gloom of your retirement years—being financially strapped, being bored, contracting a horrible disease—it detracts from the time you have to prepare for your retirement. Spend your time wisely.

Prepare now. Worrying about it isn't going to change the outcome because what is going to happen is going to happen whether you worry about it or not. But you can put plans in place and prepare now for what is to come.

This planning and positive thinking can help to alter the outcome, or at least prepare you for it.

We can re-program our minds to think positive by consciously replacing compulsive, half-empty thoughts with those likely to lead to a 'brighter' outcome. What are your goals for this free period of your life? What footprints do you wish to leave in the sand? If you have ever taken a yoga class, you have already been introduced to the power of positive thinking. Before every practice, as you are settling into self, you make a purpose for your practice. Then, you have to envision yourself fulfilling your purpose. Doing something similar for envisioning your retirement can work you toward the way of life you are seeking during retirement.

The concept of the power that positive thinking can have on your life isn't a new concept, but it was most recently revisited by the best-selling book *The Secret* by Rhonda Byrnes.

It covers how to harness positive thinking and use it in every aspect of your life -- money, health, relationships, happiness, and in every interaction you have in the world. As you progress into retirement, use the positive power within you to set and achieve your goals.

Finding your goals

As mentioned earlier, many people enter into a state of depressions when they first retire. It may not be right away. But after some leisure time has worn away, many retirees start to feel worthless. When working they had a purpose or at least something to occupy their time every day. Now, without an exact purpose, negative thoughts start to set in and it just goes downhill from there.

In order to avoid this happening to you, take some time to write out your goals and aspirations. Make sure to be as positive as possible when you are coming up with your list.

Also make sure you word your goals in a positive manner. Whether you prefer to make a paper and pen list or one on your computer, spend some time creating a plan for how you envision your retirement unfolding.

When making your list of goals, there are really two parts involved—emotional goals and financial goals. Part II of this book will help you to take a closer look at the financial aspect of retirement, but this exercise will help you work through the emotional side of retirement, which directly affects the financial part of life too. Be sure to spend some time creating goals for both aspects of your life. You can also use the following worksheet to help you create a retirement goal guideline to live by. It helps you to put your retirement goals in perspective. Putting your goals in writing pushes you toward accomplishing your goals, so make sure to write it down.

Writing your goals down also allows you to review and update your goals from time to time, and to see which goals you have achieved and which goals you may still be working towards achieving.

Retirement Goals Worksheet

Use this worksheet as a guideline for creating retirement goals and aspirations. Fill in your answers to the questions, jot down notes, make some kind of record of your goals. Make sure to write your answers in a positive way.

1. I want to spend my time (list at least three activities):
   - 1.
   - 2.
   - 3.

2. A day in the life of my retirement will look like this (not to create a rigid schedule, but paint a picture of what a day in retirement life may look like in a positive way):

3. How will these activities make me feel (list at least three adjectives)?

- 1.
- 2.
- 3.

4. How will these activities help me or help others?

- 1.
- 2.
- 3.

5. Write out three positive statements that pertain to your retirement (i.e., "I have enough money coming in to live comfortably and to share with my family and favorite charities" or "I am setting a great example for my grandchildren, sharing my best experiences and what I've have learned in life.") Statements like these will help to erase some of the negative thoughts we have swirling around in our heads.

- 1.

- 2.

- 3.

LRVs? The Right choice for me?

An LRV, or Living Retirement Village, is a community of retired people different than a nursing home. It consists of lodging similar to an apartment or condominium and only admits those either no longer working or of a certain age, generally about 55 or older.

They are built in warmer climates and have facilities built to cater to the wishes and needs of those living there; including swimming pools, clubhouses, golf courses, boating and on-site medical facilities. LRV's can also occur on a natural basis. Those who have retired and move to low-cost living areas generally find themselves amidst other retirees. There are three different types of LRV's:

- Active: there is no long-term healthcare and are known as independent living communities.

- Active/Supportive: combines both independent and long-term care and are known as continuing care retirement communities.

- Supportive: all long-term healthcare and are known as nursing homes.

Depending on the community you want to belong to, the cost differs. Research where you would like to live and what services are provided or residents have access to as a member of the community.

AM I READY TO QUIT THE RAT-RACE?

While most people look forward to retirement, others find it a scary thought to contemplate. Knowing whether or not you are actually ready to retire may mean the difference between retiring happy and being miserable. The following will help you to determine if you are mentally prepared to stop working and start living work-free.

You won't miss social interactions at work

Once you leave your job, all the bonds and friendships you have made are likely to disintegrate but if most of your social connections outside of work are still there after you leave, then leaving the work force isn't an issue.

You don't need the structures that working gives you

By this I mean that you enjoy getting up early, commuting, doing whatever menial tasks are given to you, doing repeated tasks, and then commute back home late at night. The work structure can be replaced by a new one, like getting up early, going out jogging, doing various home projects, have a nap, spend time with your loved ones and go to bed. If you can fill your schedule without having to work, it's a sign you're ready to move on.

So much to do in so little time

Working often allows people to feel busy and if they aren't busy they try and find some way to be busy. If work fills your life with lots of things to do and you're worried about not having that after you retire, consider this. Is there some project or hobby you've wanted to start or devote more time to but never had the chance to beforehand? If that's the case then there are more than enough things to do that will take up your time once you're through working.

Your health is important to you

Working day in and day out has left many people struggling with health issues like stress, high blood pressure, obesity and heart conditions. This is because they can't find a balance between work and health in order to keep living longer. By giving up demanding and stressful jobs, people find that their health gets better.

You've other income to live off of

You've saved and planned or are thinking of cutting back to a lighter, part-time job once you've retired and are able to live off those savings. If you're able to cut out your job and still live comfortably, then there's no reason you're not ready to retire.

CONCLUSION

WHERE DO I GO FROM HERE & ENJOY THOSE WONDERFUL RETIREMENT YEARS

Where you go and what you do after you retire all depends on the individual. Whether its travel, volunteering, spending time with family or friends, there's no end to what you can do once you've retired. As long as you've planned and prepared for it as best you can by budgeting, consulting with advisors, investing and comparing plans, then your golden years should be both merry and bright.

RETIREMENT-AT-A-GLANCE

This Retirement-At-A-Glance worksheet was adapted from the American Savings Education Council. It will help you tackle a subject many Americans avoid because they find it too scary or intimidating: determining how much they need to save for retirement.

By simplifying some issues that seem complicated, such as projected Social Security benefits and earnings assumptions on savings, the worksheet offers you a way to estimate what you'll need for retirement. The worksheet assumes you'll need at least 75 percent of your current income that you'll live to age 87, and you'll realize a constant real rate of return of 3 percent after inflation.

This worksheet demonstrates how easy it is to take the first step – estimating the total amount you'll need at retirement, and how much you'll need to save each month to get there.

1. How much annual income will you want for retirement? Enter the amount to the right: (Figure at least 75 percent of your current annual gross income just to maintain your current standard of living. Really.)

Annual income wanted: $\$\underline{\hspace{2cm}}$

2.   SUBTRACT the income you expect to receive annually from:

Social Security – If you are eligible to receive benefits from Social Security, you should contact the Social Security Administration at (800) 772-1213 to get your personalized statement of benefits. If you already have one, enter the appropriate dollar amount below.

REMEMBER – If you are planning to retire before the age you would be eligible for "full" benefits (varies based on the year you were born), your monthly income will be reduced. If you retire before you reach the age that you can receive the reduced amount, you will need to have other retirement income to replace this amount until you are old enough to begin to receive these benefits. If you don't have personalized Social Security information but want to get a general idea now through this Retirement-At-A-Glance worksheet, you can enter one of the following amounts:

- if you made under $25,000 while under covered employment, enter $8,000;

- between $25,000 and $40,000, enter $12,000;

- more than $40,000, enter $14,500.

Married couples should enter the benefit based on the earnings for the lower earning spouse, or 50% of the higher earning spouse's benefit (using the amounts above), whichever is higher. But, keep in mind that these amounts will not reflect the actual benefit you may receive.

- If you are not eligible for Social Security, enter $0:

$$- \quad \$\underline{\hspace{4cm}}$$

$$\text{Subtotal:} \quad \$\underline{\hspace{4cm}}$$

Enter the amount you expect to receive annually from your defined benefit plan (a plan that pays a set dollar amount for life based on your salary, age, and years of service).

Your annual retirement benefits: − $\$\underline{\hspace{3cm}}$

Subtotal: $\$\underline{\hspace{3cm}}$

Your part-time income: − $\$\underline{\hspace{3cm}}$

Other: − $\$\underline{\hspace{3cm}}$

This is how much you need to make up for each retirement year. (If your result is a negative number, congratulations. You're on the way to meeting your financial goals!)

Total to make up: $\$\underline{\hspace{2.5cm}}$

Now you want a ballpark estimate of how much money you'll need in savings on the day you retire.

3. To determine the amount you'll need to save, MULTIPLY the amount you need to make up (results of Question 2) by the factor below.

Age you expect to retire: Your factor is:

55   21.0

60   18.9

65   16.4

70   13.6

Total amount to save: $_____

4. If you expect to retire before age 65, MULTIPLY your Social Security benefit (amount from Question 2) by the factor below. (If you are not eligible for Social Security and entered $0, enter $0 here also.)

Age you expect to retire: Your factor is:

55   8.8

60   4.7

Subtotal: $_____

Subtotal of Questions 3 + 4: $_____

5. MULTIPLY any savings you have to date by the factor below (include money accumulated in a 401(k), IRA, or similar plan).

You want to retire in: Your factor is:

10 years   1.3

15 years   1.6

20 years   1.8

25 years   2.1

30 years   2.4

35 years   2.8

40 years   3.3

SUBTRACT value of current savings at retirement:

− $_____

Total savings needed at retirement: = $_____

Don't panic. Here's another formula to show you how much to save each year in order to reach your total amount needed at retirement. Factor in compounding – that's where your money not only makes interest, your interest starts making interest.

6. To determine the ANNUAL amount you'll need to save, MULTIPLY the TOTAL amount needed at retirement by the factor below.

You want to retire in: Your factor is:

You want to retire in:	Your factor is:
10 years	.085
15 years	.052
20 years	.036
25 years	.027
30 years	.020
35 years	.016
40 years	.013

TOTAL TO SAVE EACH YEAR: $_____

It just takes planning. And the sooner you start, the better off you'll be.

APPENDIX A: RETIREMENT PLANNING GLOSSARY

A

Actuary: A person who calculates risks and premiums.
Annual Return: The total return on an investment which includes dividend payments and capital.
Annuity: an investment of money entitling the investor to a series of sums over a stated period.

B

Bankruptcy: declared in law unable to pay debts
Beneficiary: a person who receives benefits under a trust, policy or will.
Benefits in kind: Benefits excluding salaries given to employees by employers i.e. car, car fuel, medical etc.

Bond: a certificate issued by a government or a public company promising to repay borrowed money at a fixed rate of interest at a specified time.

C

Capital Growth: The increase in value of an asset.
Capital Structure: The components which form a company's capital (ordinary shares, preference shares, debentures etc).

D

Decreasing term assurance: Life insurance which decreases over the term of the policy.

E

Earned Income: Income that comes from work (salary, wages).
Execution Only Broker: A broker who buys and sells shares on the instructions of clients but who offers no advice.

F

Final Salary Scheme (Defined Benefit Scheme): A pension scheme in which an employee's pension is based on number of years of service and final salary.

Financial Adviser: A professional person qualified to give advice to clients regarding a range of financial products.

Footsie: The Financial Times 100 Share Index is a measure of Britain's top 100 companies.

Fund: A stock of money.

Fund Manager: A professional person whose role is to decide how fund money is invested.

Fund Switching: The movement of money from one fund to another.

G
Gain: Acquire as profits.

H
Hang Seng Index: The main indicator of stock market performance in Hong Kong based on 33 companies.

Health Insurance: Generic term for insurance covering costs incurred due to illness or injury

Home Income Plan: A plan enabling the elderly owner of a property to utilize its capital value.

I

Index linked term assurance: Term assurance in which premiums and benefits are increased in line with a specific index.
Inheritance Tax: Tax due on an estate following the death of the owner.

J

Joint Life Assurance: An assurance policy usually taken out on two lives, typically husband and wife.

L

Lump Sum: A sum of money paid in a single installment.

M

Market Value: Value as a saleable thing.

Money: A current medium of exchange in the form of coins and banknotes.
NASDAQ: The first electronic stock market.

N

National Debt: The total debt accumulated by a government through the issue of government bonds, treasury bills etc.

Normal Retirement Age: The age at which a person normally retires.

O

Occupational Pension Scheme: A pension organized and managed by an organization for the benefit of its employees.

P

Pension Forecast: A projection of estimated pension income upon retirement.

Pension Mortgage: A pension plan which uses the lump sum to repay a mortgage.

Pension: A regular payment made to people above a certain age.
Personal Income: A person's total income.
Phased Retirement: Gradual reduction in working hours when approaching full retirement.

Q

Quartile: The investment industry divides performance into four equal groups.

Quote: An estimate of future returns.

R

Registrar of Companies: The official body with responsibility for the registration of companies.

Retire: leave office or employment

S

Safe: Not involving danger or risk.

Sale: The exchange of a commodity for money etc.

Share: a portion of an enterprise

Stock Exchange: An association of dealers in stocks and shares, conducting business according to fixed rules.

T

Take home pay: The amount of money available after all deductions from salary.

Tax avoidance: The minimizing of tax liability via legal activities.
Term: A specific period of time.

Testate: Having left a valid will at death.

Tokyo Stock Price Index: The index of the 1,000 largest companies quoted on the Tokyo Stock Exchange.

Tracker Fund: A fund which aims to achieve the same returns as a specific share index.

Trust Fund: A fund of money etc held in trust.

U

Umbrella Fund: A collective fund containing several sub-funds, each of which invests in a different asset class.

V

Valuation: The worth of a portfolio of investments.
Variable Interest Rate: The rate offered by an institution which is likely to fluctuate in line with the base rate.

W

Warrant: Securities issued by a company which give their owners the right to purchase shares in the company at a specific price at a future date.

Will: A written document usually instructing funeral wishes and how an estate is to be distributed upon death.

X
Xd: Ex dividend.

Xw: Ex warrants

Y
Year End Dividend: An additional dividend paid at the end of the trading year.

Yield: The return of money.

Z
Zero Coupon Bond: A bond which pays no interest through its life.

Zero Dividend Preference Shares: Preference shares which receive no dividend throughout their lives.

APPENDIX B: INVESTMENT GLOSSARY

A

Accumulation

This is another way of saying: professional buying. A stock is under accumulation when volume expands on days when price moves up.

Alpha

Alpha measures a stock's average monthly move over the past 12 months if the S&P 500 index is unchanged during this 12-month period. For example, a stock with a high alpha of 7 would be expected to rise 7% in a month given an unchanged S&P 500 index.

American depositary receipt

Known as ADRs, these securities are created by a U.S. bank and represent foreign securities that trade in the U.S. financial markets.

Annual report

Companies send their shareholders an annual report at the end of a fiscal year. The magazine or brochure sizes up company operations and displays earnings, sales, balance sheets, and financial footnotes.

Arbitrage

Arbitrageurs make their living by seizing on price differences for a security traded on a different market or in a different form, such as an option or a futures contract. Someone who buys, say, a soybean contract on one market and sells a soybean contract on another exchange is practicing arbitrage by locking in a profit.

Ask

This is the quoted ask, or the lowest price an investor will accept to sell a stock. Practically speaking, this is the quoted offer at which an investor can buy shares of stock.

B

Balanced mutual fund

This is a fund that buys common stock, preferred stock and bonds.

Basic earnings

A simple calculation that takes net income divided by shares outstanding to get per-share earnings.

Basis point

In the bond market, the smallest measure used for quoting yields is a basis point. One basis point is 0.01 percent of a bond's yield. Basis points also are used for interest rates. An interest rate of 5 percent is 50 basis points greater than an interest rate of 4.5 percent.

Bellwether stock

The stock of a company recognized as a leader in its industry. For example, IBM is considered a bellwether stock in the computer field. Often, the fortunes of an industry are reflected in the behavior of its bellwether stocks.

Beta

This measures the volatility of a share of stock. A high beta stock, for example, will rise more in value than the stock market average on a day when shares in general are rising. And it will fall more sharply than the average on a day when shares are falling. The Standard & Poor's 500 Index of stocks, an index that represents large-company stocks, has a beta of 1.

Bid

This is the quoted bid, or the highest price an investor is willing to pay to buy a security. Practically speaking, this is the available price at which an investor can sell shares of stock.

Bond

Bonds are debt and are issued for a period of more than one year. The U.S. government, local governments, water districts, companies and many other types of institutions sell bonds. When an investor buys bonds, he or she is lending money. The seller of the bond agrees to repay the principal amount of the loan at a specified time. Interest-bearing bonds pay interest periodically.

Book to Bill

Book to bill is the semiconductor book to bill ratio. It reports on the amount of semiconductor chips that are booked for delivery as compared with those that companies already have billed for.

Book value

A company's book value is total assets minus intangible assets and liabilities such as debt. Book value might be more or less than the market value of the company.

Breadth

This is one of those technical terms you hear in a trading room. It simply demonstrates how broadly a market is moving. When three-quarters of the stocks on the New York Stock Exchange, for example, rise during a given day, an observer might say the stock market had good breadth. Often, observers will measure the number of stocks advancing against the number declining as one way of monitoring breadth.

Buy Price

Enter here the price you paid for a security. If, for example, you paid 8 1/4 a share for a security, enter 8 1/4.

C

Call option

This security gives investors the right to buy a security at a fixed price within a given time frame. An investor, for example, might wish to have the right to buy shares of a stock at a certain price by a certain time in order to protect, or hedge, an existing investment.

Certificate of deposit

CDs, as they are called, pay interest to investors for as long as five years.

Change

This shows the change in price of a security from the previous day's closing price. For instance, -1 1/8 means the security has fallen $1.12.

Chief Operating Officer (COO)

A person who has full operational responsibilities for the day-to-day activities of an organization.

Closed-end fund

A closed-end fund sells a fixed number of shares to investors. Those shares sell on an exchange and vary in price, depending on demand for the fund. A fund's shares, for example, can trade below their net asset value or above their net asset value - depending on investors' demand for the shares. Country funds that represent shares in a specific country or region, such as Italy or France, are often closed-end funds.

Commission

This is a fee an investor pays a broker for buying or selling securities.

Commodity

A commodity is food, a metal or another physical substance that investors buy or sell, usually via futures contracts.

Common shares

These are securities that represent equity ownership in a company. Common shares let an investor vote on such matters as the election of directors. They also give the holder a share in a company's profits via dividend payments or the capital appreciation of the security.

Consumer Price Index

The CPI, as it is called, measures the prices of consumer goods and services and is a measure of the pace of U.S. inflation. The U.S. Department of Labor publishes the CPI every month.

Consumer stock

The stock of a company that produces consumer-oriented products like food, beverages, tobacco, pharmaceuticals.

Currency

This shows the currency that a security trades in, such as USD for U.S. dollar.

Current Yield

If a security has a dividend, the yield is the price of a stock dividend. A $10 stock that pays a 50 cent dividend for the year has a 5% yield.

Cyclical stock

The stock of a company whose fortunes are closely tied to the cyclical ups and downs of the economy in general. For example, General Motors is a cyclical stock since its business of selling autos is highly dependent on a robust economy with its attendant high levels of employment, rising personal incomes, etc.

D

Day High

This is the highest price that a security has traded at during the day.

Day Low

This is the lowest price that a security has traded at during the day.

Devaluation

A lowering of a country's currency relative to gold and/or currencies of other nations. The opposite is revaluation.

Debenture

The common type of bond issued by large, well-established organizations. Holders of debentures representing corporate indebtedness are creditors of the corporation and entitled to payment before shareholders upon dissolution of the corporation.

Convertible Debenture

Corporate securities (preferred shares or bonds) that are exchangeable for a set number of another form at a pre-stated price.

Subordinated Debenture

A debt that is junior in claim on assets to other debt, repayable only after other debts with a higher claim have been satisfied.

Diluted earnings

A calculation that includes stock options, warrants and convertible securities to get per-share earnings.

Discount rate

This is the interest rate charged by the U.S. Federal Reserve, the nation's central bank, for loans to member banks. The Fed, as it is called, alters rates to increase or decrease the growth of the nation's economic output.

Distribution

This is another way of saying: professional selling. A stock is under distribution when volume expands on days when price moves down.

Dividend

A dividend is a portion of a company's profit paid to common and preferred shareholders. A stock selling for $20 a share with an annual dividend of $1 a share yields the investor 5 percent.

Dow Jones Industrial Average

This is the best known U.S. index of stocks. It contains 30 stocks that trade on the New York Stock Exchange. The Dow, as it is called, is a barometer of how shares of the largest U.S. companies are performing. There are thousands of investment indexes around the world for stocks, bonds, currencies and commodities.

Duration

A measure of a bond price's sensitivity to a 100-basis point change in interest rates. A duration of 8 would mean that, given a 100-basis point change up/down in rates, a bond's price would move up/down by 8%.

E

Earnings per share (EPS)

EPS, as it is called, is a company's profit divided by its number of shares. If a company earned $2 million in one year had 2 million shares of stock outstanding, its EPS would be $1 per share.

Eurodollar

This is an American dollar that has been deposited in a European bank. It got there as a result of payments made to overseas companies for merchandise.

Ex-dividend

This literally means "without dividend." The buyer of shares when they are quoted ex-dividend is not entitled to receive a declared dividend.

EDGAR

The Securities & Exchange Commission uses Electronic Data Gathering and Retrieval to transmit company documents to investors. Those documents, which are available via DBC's Smart Edgar service, include 10-Qs (quarterly reports), 8-Ks (significant developments such as the sale of a company unit) and 13-Ds (disclosures by parties who own 5% or more of a company's shares).

Exchange

There are three main U.S. stock exchanges on which securities are traded. AMEX is the American Stock Exchange. NASDAQ is the National Association of Securities Dealers. NYSE is the New York Stock Exchange.

F

52 Week High

This is the highest price that a security has traded at during the last 52 weeks.

52 Week Low

This is the lowest price that a security has traded at during the last 52 weeks.

Federal funds rate

This is the interest rate that banks with excess reserves at a Federal Reserve district bank charge other banks that need overnight loans. The Fed Funds rate, as it is called, often points to the direction of U.S. interest rates.

Float

The so-called float is the number of shares of a security that are outstanding and available for trading by the public.

Futures contract

This is an agreement that allows an investor to buy or sell a commodity, like gold or wheat, or a financial instrument, like a currency, at some time in future. A future is part of a class of securities called derivatives, so named because such securities derive their value from the worth of an underlying investment.

G

GAAP (General Accepted Accounting Principles)
Conventions, rules and procedures that define general accounting practice, including broad guidelines as well as detailed procedures.

Growth stock

The stock of a company whose business is considered recession-resistant and also possesses an above-average growth rate.

H

High price

This is the day's highest price of a security that has changed hands between a buyer and seller.

I

Initial public offering

An IPO is stock in a company that is being traded on an exchange for the first time. Investors first read a prospectus that describes the potential of the company and the risks of investing in it.

Insiders

These are directors and senior officers of a corporation -- in effect those who have access to inside information about a company. An insider also is someone who owns more than 10 percent of the voting shares of a company.

J

Junk bond

A bond with a speculative credit rating of BB or lower is a junk bond. Such bonds offer investors higher yields than bonds of financially sound companies. Two agencies, Standard & Poor's and Moody's Investor Services, provide the rating systems for companies' credit.

K/L

Last

This indicates the most recent trade of a security.

LEAP

A LEAP is a long-term option contract for a company's stock. They usually run for one year or more and are available on several U.S. exchanges.

Limit order

Investors can place an order to buy or sell securities at a set price. The trade can take place only at that price or a lower one.

Long

Investors who go "long" simply own stock or another security. It is a term that means the opposite of "short," in which investors are short a stock or security because they have borrowed it and sold it to someone else.

Low price

This is the day's lowest price of a security that has changed hands between a buyer and a seller.

M

Margin

This allows investors to buy securities by borrowing money from a broker. The margin is the difference between the market value of a stock and the loan a broker makes.

Market Cap

This is the company's market capitalization. If a company has 10 million shares and the company's shares are selling for $10, the market cap is $100 million.

Market order

This is an order to buy or sell a security at the current trading price.

Momentum

The rate of acceleration of an economic, price or volume movement. An economy with strong growth that is likely to continue is said to have momentum.

Money market

Money markets are for borrowing and lending money for three years or less. The securities in a money market can be U.S. government bonds, Treasury Bills and commercial paper from banks and companies.

Money Supply

The stock of money in the economy, consisting of currency in circulation and deposits in checking and savings accounts. M1, M2 and M3 represent money and near-money.

Moving average

A moving average is an average of a security's price over a specific time period. The average changes, for example, on a 30-day moving average, so that it includes the most current 30 trading days. Moving averages often indicate levels of support or resistance for a security.

Municipal bond

State or local government offer municipal bonds, as they are called, to pay for special projects such as highways or sewers. The interest that investors receive is exempt from some income taxes.

Mutual fund

Mutual funds are pools of money that are managed by an investment company. They offer investors a variety of goals, depending on the fund and its investment charter. Some funds, for example, seek to generate income on a regular basis. Others seek to preserve an investor's money. Still others seek to invest in companies that are growing at a rapid pace. Funds can impose a sales charge, or load, on investors when they buy or sell shares. Many funds these days are no load and impose no sales charge.

N

Net asset value

Listed as NAV in mutual fund listings, net asset value is the market value of a fund's shares. It is calculated at the close of trading.

Net Change

This is the difference between a day's last trade and the previous day's last trade.

Net Profit

This is the difference between the total price you paid for a security, with the brokerage commission you paid, and the current value. It will show either a profit or a loss.

Number of Shares

This is the number of stock shares that a company has outstanding.

Notes

Enter here important notes, such as your reason for buying or selling a security.

NYSE Beta Index

The beta is the covariance of the stock in relation to the rest of the stock market. The Standard & Poor's stock index has a beta coefficient of 1. Any stock with a higher beta is more volatile than the market. Any with a lower beta does the reverse.

O

Open

The price at which a security opens the trading day. Generally, the opening price reflects the previous day's close -- unless extraordinary news or demand to buy or sell have occurred before the market opens.

Open-end mutual fund

A fund that sells its shares at net asset value is an open-end fund. It creates shares as investors demand them. Investors buy the shares at their market price. Most mutual funds are open-end funds. Those that aren't are closed-end funds that sell a fixed number of shares to investors.

Open order

An open order is any order to buy or sell securities that has yet to be executed.

Options

These contracts give the holder the right to buy or sell securities at a set price or a set period of time. Investors often use them to protect, or hedge, an existing investment. An option is part of a class of securities called derivatives, so named because these securities derive their value from the worth of an underlying investment.

Over-the-counter

The O-T-C market is for securities not listed on a stock exchange.

P

Pay Date

The date on which a declared stock dividend or a bond interest payment is scheduled to be paid.

Percent Change

This calculates the percentage change in the price of a security from the previous trading day's closing price.

Percent Profit

This is your profit or loss expressed as a percentage of your original investment and including the cost of your brokerage commission. If you bought 1,000 shares of a stock at $10, paid a $100 commission and saw the shares rise to $14, your percentage would be 39.6 percent.

Preferred shares

Preferred shares give investors a fixed dividend from the company's earnings. And more importantly: preferred shareholders get paid before common shareholders.

Premium

This generally refers to extra money an investor is willing to pay to buy or sell something. For a bond, a premium is the amount for which the security sells above its par value. For a stock, a premium is the amount that a security's price exceeds those of its peer group, or comparable stocks.

Previous

This is the closing price of a security from the previous trading day.

Prime Rate

The interest rate banks charge, determined by market forces affecting a bank's cost of funds and the rates the borrowers will accept. This rate tends to become standard for the banking industry when a major bank raises or lowers its rate.

P/E

A stock has a price-to-earnings ratio: the share price divided by earnings per share for the company's most recent four quarters. A projected P/E divides the share price by estimated earnings per share for the coming four quarters.

Put option

This security gives investors the right to sell fixed number of shares at a fixed price within a given time frame. An investor, for example, might wish to have the right to sell shares of a stock at a certain price by a certain time in order to protect, or hedge, an existing investment.

Q/R

Reaction

This term has been around as long as the stock market itself and is used to describe a short-term drop in prices.

Real time

A real-time stock, bond, option or futures quote is one that reports the most current price available when a security changes hands. A delayed quote shows a security's price 15 minutes and sometimes 20 minutes after a trade takes place.

Record Date

The date on which a shareholder must officially own shares in order to be entitled to a dividend. After the date of record the stock is said to be ex-dividend.

Relative Strength

Stocks which have been strong relative to all other stocks should continue to be relatively stronger in the future and securities which have been relatively weak tend to continue to be weaker.

Return on equity

Return on equity measures the return, expressed as a percentage, earned on a company's common stock investment for a specific period. It is calculated by common stock equity, or a company's net worth, into net income. The calculation is performed after preferred stock dividends and before common stock dividends. The figure shows investors how well -- how effectively -- their money is being used by managers.

S

Securities & Exchange Commission

The SEC is a federal agency that regulates the U.S. financial markets.

SEC EDGAR

The Securities & Exchange Commission uses Electronic Data Gathering and Retrieval to transmit company documents to investors. Those documents, which are available via DBC's Smart Edgar service, include 10-Qs (quarterly reports), 8-Ks (significant developments such as the sale of a company unit) and 13-Ds (disclosures by parties who own 5% or more of a company's shares).

Security
This piece of paper proves ownership of stocks, bonds and other investments.

Sell Price

Enter here the price you received when you sold a security. If you received $10 for a share that you sold at 10, then enter 10.

Settlement date

In U.S. financial markets, an investor must pay for the purchase of shares by the third business day after he or she buys securities. And an investor must deliver an investment that he or she has sold by the third business day after the transaction.

Shareholders' equity

This is a company's total assets minus total liabilities. A company's net worth is the same thing.

Shares
Enter here the number of shares you own. If you bought shares of a specific security at different times and various prices, enter the total number of shares here and enter the average price for the purchases under Buy Price.

Short sale

Investors who borrow stock and sell it to someone else are betting the shares go down in price. Then, they can buy back the stock at a lower price and pocket the difference as profit. Going "short" is the opposite of going "long," or owning shares for the long haul.

Short interest

This is the total number of shares of a security that investors have sold short -- borrowed, then sold in the hope that the security will fall in value. An investor then buys back the shares and pockets the difference as profit.

Special

CBS MarketWatch's portfolio and multiple quote pages offer special buttons that give users the choice to do more research. N = News - This function searches news sources including CBS MarketWatch and Reuters for news pertaining to the ticker symbol selected. S = SEC filings. E = Earnings information from Zacks. H = Hoover's capsules. M = MarketGuide. F = Fundamentals, such as price-earnings ratios and 52-week highs and lows. C = 180 day Chart. FP = Mutual Fund profiles.

Spinoff

A company can create an independent company from an existing part of the company by selling or distributing new shares in the so-called spinoff.

Split

Sometimes, companies split their outstanding shares into larger number of shares. If a company with one million shares did a two-for-one split, the company would have two million shares. An investor, for example, with 100 shares before the split would hold 200 shares after the split. The investor's percentage of equity in the company remains the same.

Spread

This is the gap between bid and ask prices of a stock or other security.

Stock ticker

This is a lettered symbol assigned to securities and mutual funds that trade on U.S. financial exchanges.

Symbol

This is the ticker symbol of the security. New York Stock Exchange and American Stock Exchange tickers, for example, are three or fewer letters. Example: Ford is F. Nasdaq tickers are four and sometimes five letters. Example: Data Broadcasting Corp. is DBCC. Mutual Fund tickers end with the letter "X." Options tickers have their own help tables.

T

Tick

This refers to a change in the price of a security. An uptick occurs when the last trade in a security takes place at a higher price than the prior trade. A downtick occurs when the last trade in a security takes place at a lower price than the prior trade. An indicator may be fashioned from the difference between the number of NYSE issues showing upticks on the last trade and the number of NYSE issues showing downticks on the last trade. This indicator is known as the TICK, and is found on many quote screens. A TICK of +236 means 236 more NYSE issues last traded on upticks than those trading on downticks.

Trade sizes

On most trading screens, investors can see the amount of stock available for buyers and sellers. In a stock with a bid price of 18 and an ask price of 18 1/2, for example, a trade size of 10x5 indicates that investors have bids in to buy 10 blocks of 100 shares at the price of 18. Sellers, on the other hand, are willing to sell five blocks of 100 shares at 18 1/2.

Trading halt

Trading of a stock, bond, option or future contract can be halted by an exchange while news is being broadcast about the security.

Triple-Witching

This occurs on the third Friday of March, June, September and December when futures and stock options, based on the S&P 500 index, all expire on the same day.

Turnover (Securities)

The volume of shares traded as a percentage of total shares listed on an exchange during a period, usually a day or a year. The same ratio is applied to individual securities and the portfolio of individual or institutional investors.

U

U.S. Treasury bill

U.S. government debt with a maturity that is less than a year is a bill.

U.S. Treasury bond

U.S. government debt with a maturity of more than 10 years is a bond.

U.S. Treasury note

U.S. government debt with a maturity of one to 10 years is a note.

V

Value

This is the current price of the security multiplied by the number of shares you own. If you own 1000 shares of Apple Computer, and the shares are selling for $25, the value should be $25,000.

Value stock

A stock perceived by the marketplace to be undervalued based on criteria such as its price-to-earnings ratio, price-to-book ratio, dividend yield, etc.

Volatility (Historical)

This describes the fluctuations in the price of a stock or other type of security. If the price of a stock is capable of large swings, the stock has a high volatility. The pricing of options contracts depends in part on volatility. A stock with high volatility, for example, commands higher prices in the options market than one with low volatility. Volatility may be gauged by several measures, one of which involves calculating a security's standard deviation. Stock investors sometimes prefer to measure a stock's volatility versus that of an index, such as the Standard & Poor's 500 Index. This is known as a stock's beta. A beta of 1.2 implies a stock that is 20% more volatile than the S&P 500. When the S&P rises 10%, the stock is expected to rise 12%.

Volume

This is the daily number of shares of a security that changes hands between a buyer and a seller.

W

Warrant

This piece of paper gives an investor the right to purchase securities at a fixed price within a fixed time span. Warrants are like call options, but with much longer time spans -- sometimes years.

X/Y/Z

Zero coupon bond

Such a debt security pays an investor no interest. It is sold at a discount to its face price and matures in one year or longer.